Origami: a pocket book of Oriental poetry

Melissa Davilio

This book is dedicated to
my husband, James Hart,
thank you so much for just
being you.

Table Of Contents

Chinese Literary Form

As Winter Approaches

As Winter approaches, and frost coats
the barren ground,
The last of the leaves tumble to their
demise.
I visit the site of your grave.
Canadian geese wave their goodbye
with a flap of their unfurled wings.

Dragonfly

A dragonfly hunts in an amethyst
field
Scavenging for its unwary prey
He lures me in with his flattering
words
How many victims have fallen today?

Dodoitsu

A Change Of Heart

a monarch's metamorphosis
alters our perception
of the universe
a change of heart

Her Love Requited

Her love, like a bumblebee,
arrives with a dive bomb buzz
budding like a rose petal
upon requital

Doha

And In The Gloaming

And in the gloaming, at the coming
of the night,
a moth flutters its wings, attracted to
twlight.

The Whisper Of The Whippoorwill

A whippoorwill whispers on a summer
evening,
weaving the obsidian into winding
spells.

Gogyonka

August Sun Shimmering

silver stars shimmering,
moonlight glimmering,
igniting the midnight sky –
tiny flames flickering
in two lovers' eyes

Notes Coaxed From A Cello

Notes coaxed from a cello
reverberating in yellow
echoing in an empty concert hall
slip into the rafters
where they disappear in the silence

Seagulls

Seagulls surf
the wind's waves
upon sails
stitched from feathers
to survive the swales.

Slipping Into Oblivion

sinking into oblivion
delving into the void
slipping beneath the waves
escaping reality
reclaiming sanity

Twilight Twists

Twilight twists
between the brambles,
twining it into soft silhouettes,
beneath the visage
of the rising Harvest Moon.

Go Vat

My Seeds Of Sorrow

With a candle dripping tallow
I wandered into the shallows
My seeds of sorrow I planted

In the silence of the shadows
of a landscape, sacred, hallowed
My seeds of sorrow I planted

The soft ground was barren, fallow
the soil looked sunken and sallow
My seeds of sorrow I planted

A narrow pathway I followed
in the darkness I did not wallow
My seeds of sorrow I planted

Another day of life borrowed
emerging into tomorrow
My seeds of sorrow I planted

Seashells Tumbling In The Waves

Seashells tumbling in the waves
are impossible to save
as they thrash upon the shore

Collecting foam inside their caves
delicate patterns they engrave
swirling, twirling upon the shore

Maybe the sunshine they crave
as faded pathways it paves
in the white sand of the shore

Haibun

November Storm

Harsh winds blow, hinting at the a
pproach of Winter, forewarning of
the frigid nights to come, the arrival
of the sleet and snow, while
desiccated leaves scatter in the
barren fields, scraping along the soil
and the pebbles, pumpkins
perilessly perch upon front stoops, as
feisty flames roar in fireplaces

empty boughs bending
frozen icicles formed from
icy arctic blasts

Reflections

The whisper of delicate wings sings upon the breeze of a glorious August morning, storm clouds forming in the distance. Dew drops glisten as they cling to each blade of emerald grass. Beneath a willow tree I listen to the soft whoosh of the wind. Discover its revelations through the subtle susurations of my backyard garden.

dragonfly rests
on Buddha's statue ~
meditation

Lost in reverie beneath the willow tree I contemplate the things that are out of my control, the chaos of my cluttered life, the unnecessary strife collected in my soul. I am weary, yet I am leery of letting go. What am I without all of my troubles? They double for a personality. The reality of my existence. This resistance to unfold before I collapse. Perhaps, Mother Nature has better things in store for me, things I cannot see, for I have not yet discovered my own path. The aftermath of being shattered, scattered into strewn pieces of broken glass. Alas, there is a certain beauty in the pain. Even rain has a purpose. On the surface I remain focused, as placid and serene as a pond.

reflecting
beauty of the soul
a broken mirror

Haiku

A Fragile Woman

a fragile woman
standing at an open grave
yellow rose petals

A German Shepherd

a german shepherd
paddling in a swimming pool
dog days of summer

A Kaleidoscope

a kaleidoscope
of butterflies
hope for the future

Alien Beings

alien beings
hurtling through the cosmos –
discovery of man

Ancient Aliens

ancient aliens
the architects of nature
bearing the world's weight

An Empty Bench

an empty bench
on the street corner
passersby

A Phoenix Rising

a phoenix rising
from the smoldering ash
reincarnation

A Plague Of Pigeons

a plague of pigeons
pounding the pockmarked pavement
searching for breakfast

A Robin Chirping

a robin chirping
upon the break of dawn
forgiveness

A School Of Bass

a school of bass
in the pond
lily pads growing

A Scurrying Squirrel

a scurrying squirrel
searching for acorns –
plundered pine needles

A Tequila Sun

a tequila sun
intoxicates the desert –

dawn in death valley

A Whippoorwill

a whippoorwill
echoing in the dark
sound of a broken heart

A Woman

a woman
dressed in white –
decadent fantasy

Bald Eagle Soaring

bald eagle soaring
above the river
patriotic wings

Blue Orchids

blue orchids
in a crystal vase,
displaced sorrow

Boulders

boulders
covered with moss –

hidden emotions

Bumblebee Buzzing

bumblebee buzzing
near the bushes
hostas in bloom

Butterflies Flutter

butterflies flutter
in a grassy field
wildflowers grow

Calico Kitten

calico kitten
climbing up a tall tree
curiosity

Caterpillars Crawling

caterpillars crawling
in the grass –
caricatures of cabooses

Chartreuse Blades Of Grass

chartreuse blades of grass
growing like fertilized weeds
manicured front lawn

Cherry Blossoms

cherry blossoms
fuchsia florets bursting
into elegance

Coral Kasumi

coral kasumi
the tangerine sun veiled
with delicate lace

Coral Sunset

52

coral sunset ~
coronet crowning
cobalt sky

Cricket Chirping

cricket chirping
why must you

torment me so

Crimson Sun

54

crimson sun
collapsing into a pond
the lilting of a loon

Crinkled Wrinkles

crinkled wrinkles
cracks in the plaster of
an unpainted wall

Curtains Framing

curtains framing
a closed window
collecting dust

Dead Roses

dead roses
crinkled love letters
tossed into the trash

Delicate Daisies

delicate daisies
dotting a meadow
kindred spirits

Dew Drops

dew drops –
a proud mother
gently weeping

Distant Memories

distant memories
captured on the mind's film reel –

documentaries

Downward Facing Dog

downward facing dog
reclining on the couch
with my puppy

Downy Bits Of Wings

downy bits of wings
floating towards the heather
wispy, airy things

Dragonflies Darting

dragonflies darting
among the dandelions
grassy knoll in spring

Emerald Dragon

emerald dragon
guarding fairy tale turrets
silent sentinel

Family Gathered

family gathered
around the dinner table

four generations

Fresh Air

fresh air
a dolphin surfaces
to breathe

Fresh Vegetables

fresh vegetables
plucked from my garden
cornucopia

Garish Butterfly

garish butterfly –
how I long
to share your wings

Giggles Erupting

giggles erupting
from the mouth of a baby
tickled pink

Grains Of Sand

grains of sand
upon a beach –
encapsulated moments

Gray Pebbles Polished

gray pebbles polished
by a mountain stream –
fragments of dreams

Grey Clouds

grey clouds –
thunderstorm
on the horizon

Hydrangea Blooms

hydrangea blooms
baby blue bouquet bunches
resembling bonnets

Labyrinthine Roots

labyrinthine roots
twining beneath the surface
covert connections

Lady's Mantle Blossoms

lady's mantle blossoms
bursting from thin stems
dainty citrine crowns

Little Boy

little boy
skipping pebbles
four plinks and a plop

Lost Soul

a morning dove strolls
alone upon the asphalt
another lost soul

Maple Leaves

maple leaves
a barren bough
snaps in the wind

Monarch Butterfly

monarch butterfly
afloat among the daisies,
dainty gypsy queen

Moonlight

moonlight
blooming in wisps
a cottonfield

Moonlight Gleaming

moonlight gleaming
in the darkness –
titian titan

Mushroom Cloud Monday

mushroom cloud Monday
steel gray chaos ensuing
as alarm bell rings

My Laptop

my laptop
splayed wide open –
empty pages

Oak Leaves Falling

oak leaves falling
to the barren ground
surrendering to winter

Obsidian Rose

obsidian rose
tossed upon marble casket
fate sealed with a kiss

Old Woman Gazing

old woman gazing
into a rust framed mirror

inward reflection

On A Nature Hike

on a nature hike
caravan of ants
traipsing tiny trails

Planetary Dance

planetary dance
in oscillating orbits –
celestial sashays

Pink Peony

pink peony
blossoms like frilled faces
peeking up at me

Pumpkins

pumpkins
in a patch
jack-o'-lanterns

Puppy Love

puppy love
the memory
of a first kiss

Purple Flowers

purple flowers
bordering a grassy knoll
lavender lilies

Purple Pansies

purple pansies
in a grassy field –
photographs of Spring

Purple Petals

purple petals
with citrine centers –
sunsets in amethyst

Purple Wildflowers

purple wildflowers
blossoming in early Spring –
blotches of spilled ink

Rain Trickling

rain trickling
from the clouds
puddles of dew

Red Rose Petals

red rose petals
strewn among the cobblestones
two lovers embrace

Red Roses

red roses
embellishing a trestle
flowery prose

Rocks

rocks
in random formations
pebbles of thought

Rocks Covered With Moss

rocks covered with moss
winding to the river bank
giant stepping stones

Salmon Colors Seeping

salmon colors seeping
into alabaster sky
morning doves arrive

Seagull Swept Skyline

seagull swept skyline
spraypainted in tangerine –
sunset by the sea

Seashells Tumbling

seashells tumbling
in the waves –
shards of broken glass

Seven Crows

seven crows
cross the night sky –
dark shadows

Silken Moonlight

silken moonlight
slivers of silver
sluiced in saffron

Silver Coated Bark

silver coated bark
dappled and spotted in black
speckled birch tree limbs

Sky Painted Pink

sky painted pink
at sunset
cotten candy clouds

Spirits Of The Wood

spirits of the wood
lurking in mist shrouded trees
rustling of the leaves

Stencils Of Koi

stencils of koi
swimming in circles
imaginary pond

Sugar Magnolia

sugar magnolia
magenta blossoms
into flowers

Sultry Sun

sultry sun
setting over a silver pond
the lilting of a loon

Sunflowers

sunflowers
bowing in the breeze

harvest blessings

The Shadow

the shadow
of a praying mantis –
looming cloud

The Silhouette

the silhouette
of a pale planet –
galaxian goddess

The Sound

the sound
of rustling leaves
whispers

Tangerine And Oolong

tangerine and oolong
tempted tastebuds –

tea party

Vanilla Clouds

vanilla clouds
afloat in an azure sky

luxurious pillows

Vegetables Plucked

vegetables plucked
from vines –
harvest vignette

Water Cascading

water cascading
over moss-laden pebbles
forest in full bloom

Waves Crashing

waves crashing
upon a rocky shore
thunder

Whispers In The Night

whispers in the night
a cricket chirping beneath
my windowsill

White Linen Blossoms

white linen blossoms
poised upon petulant stems
wild summer orchids

Wildflowers Blowing

wildflowers blowing
in a field painted in jade
a tribe of gypsies

Willow Tree Budding

willow tree budding
at the onset of spring
a robin sings

Winding Words Woven

winding words woven
into expressive phrases
poetic verses

Words

words
unspoken –
thoughts

Words In Anger

words in anger
hurled –
tossed stones

Yellow Striped Snake

yellow striped snake
forked tongue flickering
to test the air

Imayo

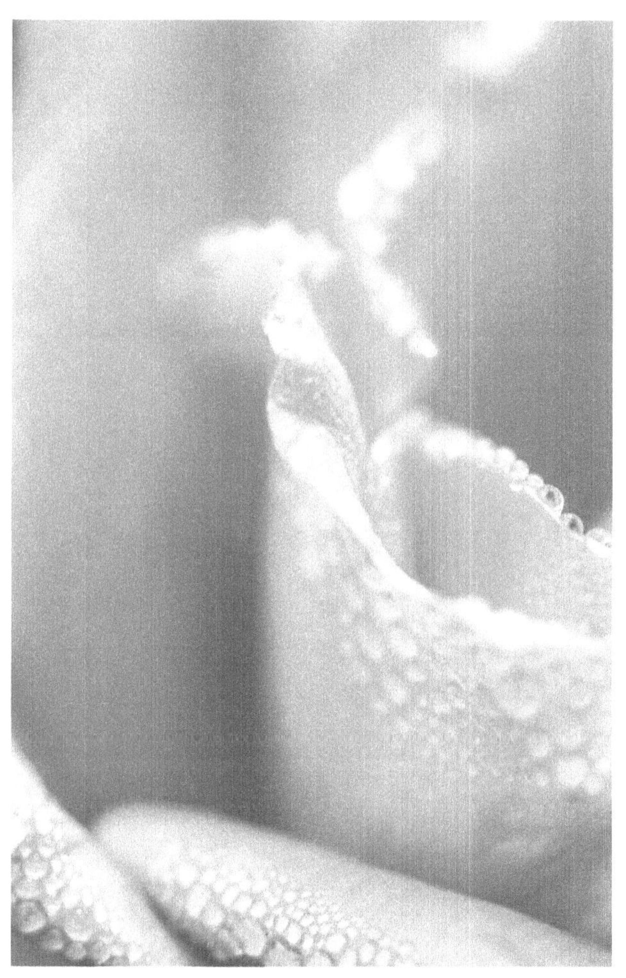

Crystalline Waves

breaching a white sandy beach
crystalline waves
within my reach seashells tumbking
I'm but a voyeur watching in f
ascination
barefooted whispers splashing
susurrations

Obsidian Night

stars glimmering a shimmer in the sky
the face of the moon a guardian bright
painted black the obsidian night
simple perfection garnering my

attention

Kimo

Azure Skyline

azure skyline painted in tangerine
transforming the horizon
upon the sun's demise

True Royalty

monarch butterfly's metamorphosis
transcendent transformation
behold true royalty

Luc Bat

At Dawn

the chillier weather
the smell of a leather jacket
stark oak tree silhouettes
the twirling pirouettes of leaves
fluttering in the breeze
the distant memory of you
'neath a sky baby blue
my heart breaking in two at dawn

Come Dawn

early Spring morning scene,
field painted tangerine, green grass
loaded with sassafras
rejuvenating fast in May,
bluebirds chatter away
at the start of the day, come dawn

Pantoum

An Avalanche Of Autumn Leaves

An avalanche of Autumn leaves
dangling from striated branches
in a forest filled with oak trees
billowing in the blowing breeze

Dangling from striated branches
pirouetting as they plummet
billowing in the blowing breeze
colors strident as a trumpet

Pirouetting as they plummet
in a forest filled with oak trees
colors strident as a trumpet
an avalanche of Autumn leaves

Violets

A field of violets in bloom
woven tapestry, verdant, lush
lavender staving off the gloom
enigmatic amethyst plush

Woven tapestry, verdant, lush
twining between the blades of grass
enigmatic amethyst plush
a winding ocean wide and vast

Twining between the blades of grass
lavender staving off the gloom
a winding ocean wide and vast
a field of violets in bloom

Pantun

Ocean Waves

How do the waves in the ocean
as they roil and cast their spray
handle all the turmoil and
commotion?

Maybe they just prefer it that way.

In The Midst Of A Stoic Universe

Oh, how I wonder if magic exists
when so much of our lives seems
cursed –
but then the beauty of the world
persists
in the midst of a stoic universe

Pathya Vat

A Summer Storm

sky painted red
in the twilight
coming of night
storm clouds forming

raindrops falling
without warning
thunder roaring
crack of lightning

Introspection

the mirror casts
her reflection –
imperfections
exposed to all

introspection
tears down her walls
removes the pall
that hides her face

Onset Of Spring

onset of spring
wildflowers grow
in a meadow
beside the brook

fern fronds nestled
in mossy nooks
I read my book
upon a rock

bees bumble by
to the tick tock
of the sun's clock
in the morning

Sedoka

A Harbor Sunset

a harbor sunset
sea gulls speckling the sky line
as they dart beneath the waves

acrylic painting
of a dock beside the bay
illustrates the entire scene

As I Miss You

Storm clouds loom
dark in the distance
over choppy waters

From red-rimmed eyes
teardrops glisten
as I stand beside your grave

A Sparrow

Storm clouds loom
dark in the distance
over choppy waters

From red-rimmed eyes
teardrops glisten
as I stand beside your grave

Flood Waters

Flood waters threaten to collapse
the levee holding them back
Its cement walls begin to crack

Teardrops well in my eyes
spilling out the sides onto my cheeks
hinting at the sorrow that I keep
buried deep

Gypsy Wildflower

gypsy wildflower
gently blowing in the breeze
on a summer afternoon

traipsing through the grass
barefoot on a pebble path
I long to be just like you

Oak Leaves Falling

oak leaves falling
to the barren ground
surrendering to winter

with a rustle
in which I hear you
whispering goodbye

Red Rosebud Blossoms

red rosebud blossoms
bursting forth from thorn lined stems
scarlet petals picked and plucked

like crimson kisses
planted upon puckered lips
destroying our innocence

Sparrow

Sparrow perched upon thin branch
wings outspread
singing to the sun

Lovely lullaby
once I sung
while I rocked your cradle

Warm Summer Breeze

warm summer breeze
blowing gently through the trees
susurrations barely heard

childhood lullabies
are alibis intended
to protect our innocence

Senryu

Acceptance Is Key

acceptance is key
to unlocking sealed up doors
positivity

Bombastic Words

bombastic words
sputtering from tight pursed lips
campaign slogans

Campaign Slogans

campaign slogans
with slick intentions
weak rhetoric

Conventional Speech

conventional speech
nefariously perverted
crowd engaged

Crowd Engaged

crowd engaged
by spewing their rage
bombastic words

Dust Seems To Settle

dust seems to settle
in the corners where it hides
among the cobwebs

Terse Phrases

terse phrases
on a teleprompter

conventional speech

Weak Rhetoric

weak rhetoric
intending to offend

terse phrases

Sijo

Lost

Lost in a forest of loneliness isolated
and alone
When breaking the silence the sound
of a cuckoo calling
Reminds me I am not broken just a
bit bruised from falling

Storm

Tyrranical thundercloud torrential
downpour threatening
Crashing into Autumn leaves
thrashing outstretched branches
Variegated avalanches tumble the
frost laden ground

Summer Storm

white capped waves thrash as the
thunder crashes and the lightning
flashes
threatening to drown the levee with
their violent smashing -
the fury of the storm silently subsides
with its passing

Somonka

The Fragrance

the fragrance
of a red rose bouquet
pales in comparison
to your perfume
scented kiss

even the dove
misses the sparrow
in the winter
waiting for the bliss
of the coming spring

Will I Hear You Whisper?

Will I hear you whisper?
feel the touch of your lips
gently placed upon mine -
delicate butterfly wings
grazing tulip blossoms

Like rose petals
puckering in the Spring
our two hearts will meet,
bumblebees in the brambles
buzzing together as one

Tanka

An Orange Butterfly

an orange butterfly
rests its wings
upon a blade of grass
as delicate as the breath
of a newborn baby

A Soft Wind Blows

a soft wind blows
through the trees
billowing leaves
dangle in the air
like exhaled breaths

Clouds Drifting

clouds drifting
in the cobalt cavern
of a cruelly callous sky
remind me of

your unforgiving face

Coral Kasumi Blooms

coral kasumi blooms
lined with pink and puce
delicate, fragile, frail
newborn baby inhales
first exquisite breath

Desiccated Leaves

desiccated leaves
flutter to the ground
on an autumn day
tiny tumbling acrobats
spiralling towards decay

Elongated Dreams

elongated nights
faded, gray-washed days
fuyu arrives on somber clouds
snowflakes enshroud the ground
isolating me in darkness

Fingertips Trailing

Fingertips as delicate as fern fronds
trailing down an achy back
bringing comfort to a weary heart
like the softness of a first kiss
Bliss in the tenderness of a touch

Forest

forest filled with trees
bearing velvet canopies
with jade colored leaves
cascading over the ground
tiny tumbling acrobats

Forest Blooming

forest blooming
into crooked perfection
draws my attention

the blush of her cheeks
stunning as she smiles

Forest Flora Blooms

forest flora blooms
with imperfect perfection
draws my attention

her blushing porcelain cheeks
pulled into a pretty smile

Joining Of Hands

joining of hands
while vows are promised
dots connected
separate paths that merge
into one

Leaves Painted Crimson

leaves painted crimson
dangling upon tree branches
tumbling in clustered
avalanches to the ground
threatening me with winter

Like A Caterpillar

like a caterpillar
alone in its cocoon,
weeping softly in the darkness,
I long to bloom,
burst forth and emerge anew

Moonlit Shadows Stretching

moonlit shadows stretching
into elongated forms
distant memories
monochrome photographs

fractured fragments from the past

Pale Fragments

pale fragments
gathered into a collection
of memories
your fragile ego
snips me out of each photograph

Pall Draped Coffin

pall draped coffin
shroud of darkness
blanketing your body
keeping you from me
forever

Pink Cherry Blossoms

pink cherry blossoms
dangling above my forehead
sweet scent of flowers
potent puffs of her perfume
captivating my senses

Replaying Our History

replaying our history
lost in its mystery
when did you disappear?
fading away,
like my breath on the Winter air

Silver Stars Shimmering

silver stars shimmering,
glittering, glimmering
igniting the midnight sky
tiny flames flickering

in two lovers' eyes

Snowflakes Glisten

snowflakes glisten as they fall
tumble to the ground
with a whisper
so many verses spoken
leaving me enthralled

The Crystalline Clarity

the crystalline clarity
of your cobalt eyes
mirrors the beauty
of a misty

mountain lake

The Wind Blowing

the wind blowing
rustling of leaves in the breeze
crinkled paper sheaves
empty pages in my notebook
desiccated, barren, blank

Tranquil Waves

tranquil waves
cascading a rocky shore
flecks of frothy foam
reminiscent of the tears
I wept upon your grave

Unkai Threaten

unkai threaten
over choppy waters,
from red-rimmed eyes
teardrops glisten
as I stand beside your grave

Violet Tendrils

violet tendrils
tucked into the horizon
as the summer sun sinks
cozy as kittens nestled
beneath warm blankets

Weep Not In Sorrow

Weep not in sorrow
for even snowflakes
cease to glisten
before seeping into the soil
at the onset of Spring

Winter Solstice Bells

winter solstice bells
ring in the darkness of night
hinting at the light
on the precipice of dawn –
celebrating survival

Winter Wind Whispers

Winter wind whispers
through the limbs of an oak tree
releasing strained sigh

boughs creaking 'neath the weight of
thickly layered ice and snow

Than Bauk

In Quarantine

in quarantine
tangerine suns
set lean and long

standing strong by
belonging here
today there's change

it's clearly strange
rearrange to
help strangers live

it's a given
proclivity
commonly shared

to be in doubt
without shouting
about our fears

I Stretched My Wings

I stretched my wings
so I'd sing proud
with ringing voice

made my choices
rejoice I'm free
you'll hear me now

I'll be less mild
like a child filled
with wild intent

so I went where
I'm meant to shine
true to thine self

Zappai

Delving Into Infinity

delving into infinity
exploring the galaxy –

uninhabited stars

Hot Air Balloons

Clouds, pink and puce,
over a field painted chartreuse –
perforated by hot air balloons

Icicles Dangling

icicles dangling
shimmering diamond marquees
from snow covered trees

Icicles Melting

icicles melting
cracked into jagged pieces
shards of broken glass

Planets Circling In Orbit

planets circling in orbit
floating through outer space

captives of their galaxies

The Moth And His Flame

wings seared to ashes
during fated lovers' tryst

love always bears risk